LET THE JOURNEY BEGIN!

Spending Detox Journal to Freedom:

Money on a Mission

by

Charity A. Morris

SPENDING DETOX JOURNAL TO FREEDOM

Money on a Mission

CHARITY A. MORRIS

21-Day Spending Detox:
Reset to Gain and Maintain Financial Freedom

Copyright 2022 © Charity A. Morris

Published by
Scribe Publications, Inc.
609-961-1755
www.scribepublicationsinc.com

ISBN-13: 979-8-9853854-4-1

Library of Congress Control Number: 2022916451

Printed in the United States of America

Table of Contents

PERSEVERANCE

NOUN

STEADFASTNESS IN DOING
SOMETHING DESPITE
DIFFICULTY OR DELAY IN
ACHIEVING SUCCESS.

Welcome to you 2.0.

I'm so excited that you are taking back control of your life and finances. You are not turning over a new leaf but starting a new one which will eventually grow into a thriving tree that will produce much healthy fruit.

You have made a quality decision to be an agent of change. With this decision comes the need to fully expose where you are in this moment. It's important to be real in your present reality. Even if it's rough, rugged, and raw or blooming like roses, facing your truth square in the eyes is necessary to make adjustments. You can't change what you're not willing to face.

BREATHE. You've got this. Whether ugly or beautiful, it will get better. Don't become overwhelmed and feel like you must do it all at one time. Pace yourself. As you journal your journey, remember to give yourself grace. Forgive yourself. Give yourself permission to heal and grow.

In my book, 21-Day Spending Detox, I walk you through ways to not only put the brakes on spending but shift your mindset from being a consumer to being a producer who builds a long-lasting legacy for generations to come. So let the journey to wellness and wealth begin!

You will not save money when you get that raise.

You will not save money when that car is paid off.

You will not save money when the kids are grown.

You will only save money when it becomes a priority.

Looking Back to Move Ahead

To effectively move forward with a clear, succinct plan, you must look back at what led to your current state. Financially, doing a postmortem on your spending helps to provide a transparent, unbiased view into your spending habits.

Typically, reviewing your spending for the month is a good start. However, for maximum effect and a full 'colonoscopy' type of deep dive into your spending trend, I recommend a six-month review. This will give you a transparent assessment of your spending trends.

As you review your spend, I recommend you categorize each transaction. Possible spend categories could include:

- Housing
- Food (groceries)
- Food (restaurant)
- Transportation
- Utilities
- Healthcare
- Debt
- Charitable Contributions
- Personal Care
- Health Care
- Savings
- Work
- Education
- Clothing
- Entertainment

ACTION: List every spending transaction for the month. *MARK "X" FOR EACH SPEND THAT IS AN ESSENTIAL NEED: Food (grocery shopping), housing, utilities, transportation, clothing (uniforms).*

Date	Item	Amount Spent	Category	Essential Need

Go to www.21DaySpendingDetox.com to download the worksheet.

TIPS

- Living in an _expensive_ apartment/home is a want. If you could save a few hundred dollars monthly by living in a more reasonably priced place, those funds will add up over the years.
- Lower costs for utilities by shopping around for your electricity (many cities have more than one option), going green with energy efficient appliances and solar panels, and using alternatives to traditional home security (Ring and Nest).
- In lieu of dining out, find a copycat recipe from your favorite restaurant and challenge yourself to find at least one coupon for your groceries (couponing is still a thing!).
- If you are driving because taking public transportation is not comfortable, that's a want. Also, consider becoming a one-car-household.
- Leverage your employer to "pay yourself first," where you deposit funds into your savings and investment accounts first. Some companies even provide opportunities to purchase life, auto and home insurance through their discounted program. You are "paying" your future self by saving for your long-term needs and expenses before paying other bills.

RECOMMENDED RESOURCES

Books

- <u>Smart is the New Rich: Money Guide for Millennials</u>, by Christine Romans

- <u>Why Didn't They Teach Me This in School? 99 Personal Money Management Principles to Live By</u>, by Cary Siegel

- <u>Simple Money: A No-Nonsense Guide to Personal Finance</u>, by Tim Maurer

Websites

- <u>Investopedia</u>

- <u>Acorns</u>

APP

- <u>Mint</u>

Your best line of
defense is truth.

Arm yourself with it,

at all times, at all
costs.

Your Money Mindset

Shifting your mind about anything, especially money, is almost as big of an effort as redirecting the Titanic. In many ways, our mind is like that iceberg, where we are only consciously minded of what we can see and touch, which is about 10%. However, it's the 90% of our iceberg mindset that's below the surface (our subconscious) that we tend to leave unaddressed. This 90% encapsulates our fundamental values, experiences, beliefs, emotions, and habits.

What you spend your money on can leave a trail of breadcrumbs to discover your true thoughts, feelings, and relationship with money. Your money mindset is a manifestation of your attitudes and beliefs about money. Whether positive or negative, it is shaped and sustained by a combination of past experiences and beliefs passed onto you by those who were an authority or influence in your life (parents, friends, leaders, clergy, social media, etc.).

A positive money mindset (along with corresponding behaviors) will navigate you towards financial freedom, Conversely, a negative money mindset is a breeding ground to produce equally negative effects.

Until you take the time to explore and investigate your thoughts, feelings, and emotions around money (and everything else in life but for now, we will focus on finances), then your subconscious mind and unconscious bias will continue to dominate your actions and ultimately your life.

The beautiful thing is that your mindset is subject to change by the inputs you feed it. Learn the lessons from the past, deprogram the negative thinking and reprogram your mind to think AND believe that abundance is attainable.

ACTION: Answer the following questions:

Do you believe your money mindset is positive or negative? Why?

_____

_____

_____

Who do you believe helped to shape it?

_____

_____

_____

How do you tend to react when you receive extra money? What do you do with it?

_____

_____

_____

Money is… (list several work associations).

_____

_____

_____

Fill in the blank: If I had more _____, I would be able to create more wealth.

> a. Expertise
> b. Resources
> c. Confidence
> d. Luck

The reason(s) I can't or may never become wealthy are…

_____

_____

_____

Rich people are…

_____

_____

_____

My greatest worries and fears regarding money and wealth are…

_____

_____

_____

Money mindset quiz

This is a simple assessment to understand your core beliefs on finances. The first step to making any change is awareness of your dominant thoughts and beliefs.

As you answer the questions, give the first answer that comes to your mind, as there is no right or wrong answer.

For each statement, rank yourself from 1 to 5, with the range of 1 = 100% Disagree to 5 = 100% Agree.

1. I believe I can be rich. All I need is a big break. ___
2. It takes money to make money.___
3. The only reason I work is to make money.___
4. Having a lot of money is a sign of greed.___
5. I can't get rich doing exactly what I love.___
6. Getting rich is a matter of chance.___
7. Realistically, it's likely that I will never be rich.___
8. If I'm rich, people will expect something from me.___
9. Investing is for rich people.___
10. I am comfortable and have the money I need.___
11. I don't feel in control of my money.___
12. There is no need to push myself to get more.___
13. I will feel at peace when I have more money.___
14. I feel pessimistic about my financial future.___
15. I tend to procrastinate with financial decisions.____
16. Getting rich takes too much work.____
17. I deserve what I have and nothing more.____
18. I sometimes think I will never get out of debt.____
19. Money will never be my friend.____
20. The rich get richer.___

Review the statements that you rated 3 and above. These are areas of opportunity to improve your money mindset.

TIPS

- Ignoring a negative thought does not make it go away. Address it by:
  - acknowledging it as such,
  - own that this is an area to grow and develop,
  - write down three statements that will debunk that thought or fear.
  - physically release it through a workout, dancing, or some other physical movement.
- Write a letter to your future self, dating it a year from now, celebrating all that you will accomplish. You are casting vision and programming your mind for success.

RECOMMENDED RESOURCES

Books

- The Money Mindset Course by Sarah Walton
- Mind over Money by Claudia Hammond
- Unlock Your Mind, Unlock Your Money by Derek J. Love
- Millionaire Mindset and Success Habits by H.J. Chammas

"Don't be pushed around by fears in your mind. Be led by the dreams in your heart."
~Roy T. Bennett

Show Up for YOU!

With the rise of stress from the hustle and bustle of life, the growing need to take care of yourself actively and intentionally in a way that supports a healthy mind, body, soul, and spirit is critical. When you show up for yourself, you choose to love and accept yourself unconditionally. You have your own back. You are your biggest advocate! And until you show up for yourself, you are unable to show up for others fully and authentically.

How you show up for yourself leads to how you show up in the world, and eventually how others show up for you. In essence, you are showing people how to treat you by how you treat yourself.

It all begins with how you love and respect yourself. Only from the overflow of a healthy, healed heart and mind can you give authentic value.

So, forgive yourself for every mistake. Accept every flaw. Love every quirky thing about you. Be unapologetically YOU! Own it! Embrace it. Come to love it.

Every freckle!

Every love handle!

Every gray hair!

Every inch of your stature!

Every loud laugh!

Every rhythmless dance!

REPEAT AFTER ME:

Today I decide to love myself enough to:

- Take back my power

- Let go of the past

- Forgive myself

- Believe what God says about me

- Get to know my authentic self and truly speak what I want and need from myself and others

- Speak well of myself

- Speak to myself with honor, respect, and dignity because I matter

- Hold myself accountable

- Step out of the zone of mediocrity and ordinary

- Know that I am worthy enough to invest in the relationship I have with myself

- Set and maintain boundaries, saying no when needed

- Practice self-compassion, extending grace to ME.

- Feel my emotions instead of avoiding or running from them

- Unapologetically REST

- Honor my purpose by fulfilling it

- Give my mind, body, soul, and spirit the peace it needs

ACTION: Answer the following questions:

What is your favorite part of your personality?

_____

_____

_____

_____

_____

What do you think others admire about you?

_____

_____

_____

_____

_____

Describe the last time you were truly happy?

_____

_____

_____

_____

_____

What's your least favorite food?

_____

_____

_____

_____

Describe your ultimate vacation.

_____

_____

_____

_____

What do you love to do for fun?

_____

_____

_____

_____

What do you do during your "me" time?

_____

_____

_____

_____

What is your personal mantra?

_____

_____

_____

_____

What are your dreams?

_____

_____

_____

_____

Describe your perfect weekend.

_____

_____

_____

_____

What are you passionate about?

_____

_____

_____

_____

What do want to accomplish in the next 1,3, and 5 years?

_____

_____

_____

_____

What does happiness look like for you?

_____

_____

_____

_____

Describe your ideal romantic relationship.

_____

_____

_____

_____

Three things I love about me are:

1._____

_____

2._____

_____

3._____

_____

TIPS

- Make time for activities that bring you peace and joy.
- Do not be dismissive of yourself. Acknowledge and honor your feelings.
- Set firm boundaries with yourself, for yourself and others.
- Stay connected with your authentic self by being honest and transparent with YOURSELF on what you want and need in life.
- Take notice of not only how you spend your money, but also how you spend your time and energy.
  - Things and people who drain or devalue you
- Don't wait for someone else to affirm you. AFFIRM AND ACKNOWLEDGE YOUR GREATNESS DAILY!
- At the end of each day, tell yourself something good that happened during your day.

RECOMMENDED RESOURCES

Books

- Agent You by Nicole Lynn
- Speak: Find Your Voice by Tunde Oyeneyin
- Own Your Greatness by Dr. Lisa Orbé-Austin
- Get Out of Your Own Way by Mark Goulston

I CHOOSE...

To live by choice, not by chance
To be motivated, not manipulated
To be useful, not used
To make changes, not excuses
To excel, not compete
I choose self-esteem, not self-pity
I choose to listen to that inner still
small voice, and not the loud
random opinions of others.

The Whys Have It

Imagine your life if you didn't have to work and had unlimited money. What would you do? Where would you go? Who would you dream of becoming now that money is no longer a factor? Why would you fulfill that mission / goal?

More than money, most people have a deep desire for the autonomous lifestyle that money brings… time to pursue passions, freedom to follow purpose, the ***choice*** to work, the leisure to travel whenever, wherever, and however they want.

Without a connected 'why' beyond 'I want money because I don't want to be broke,' you jeopardize being controlled by the magnetic pull of craving money – endlessly wanting more and more but never obtaining enough (according to your standards). This aligns with John Rockefeller's response when asked how much money was enough, "just a little more." This mentality will lure you away from your 'why' and the core of who you are.

ACTION: Answer these questions.

What would life feel and look like if you no longer had to work for money?

_____

_____

_____

_____

_____

What is financial freedom to you?

_____

_____

_____

_____

_____

What does your dream lifestyle require?

_____

_____

_____

_____

_____

How much should you have in your bank account to make that possible?

_____

_____

_____

_____

_____

What age is the deadline to save that amount?

_____

_____

_____

_____

_____

Once you find your 'why,' create a visual reference to keep in front of you, in a place where you will see it daily. Better known as a vision board, this is an excellent creative way to project your goals in pictorial form, so that every time you see that board, it will remind you of what is most important. It's an illustrative representation of what that accomplished goal looks like.

I find words and pictures from magazines, newspapers, and websites of what moves me towards success. The process of making my vision board helps to plant my goals and purpose in my head to keep me inspired and focused on my intentions, while ensuring I continue to move towards those things, both consciously and unconsciously.

ACTION: Create a vision board with images that represent each of your goals. Put the board in a place where you can see it daily.

Materials needed:
- Poster board
- Magazines
- Images and words from artworks, old books, or printed from websites
- Scissors
- Glue sticks

1. Take a moment of self-reflection and figure out what's most important to you. Set these as your goals.

2. Look through magazines and newspapers to find visual representations of your goal.
3. Arrange and affix your clippings to the board.
4. Place your vision board in a place that's within your regular line of sight to see it as often as possible.
5. Use your vision board as a road map to create an action plan
6. Review and revise the board and action plans as needed.
7. Check off those things you accomplish
8. Make more vision boards as needed. IT'S TIME TO DREAM AGAIN!

TIPS

- When working on your 'why,' think about what you're currently doing, then ask yourself "Can I see myself continuing this work years into the future? Does that excite me? "
- In addition to magazines, Google, Etsy, and Pinterest are great online resources for pictures and phrases for your vision board.

RECOMMEND RESOURCES
Website
- Dreams Alive (coaching and consulting to help manifest your personal and professional aspirations)

Books
- Start with Why by Simon Sinek
- Adulting 101 by Josh Burnette & Pete Hardesty
- Big Dreams, Daily Joys by Elise Blaha Cripe

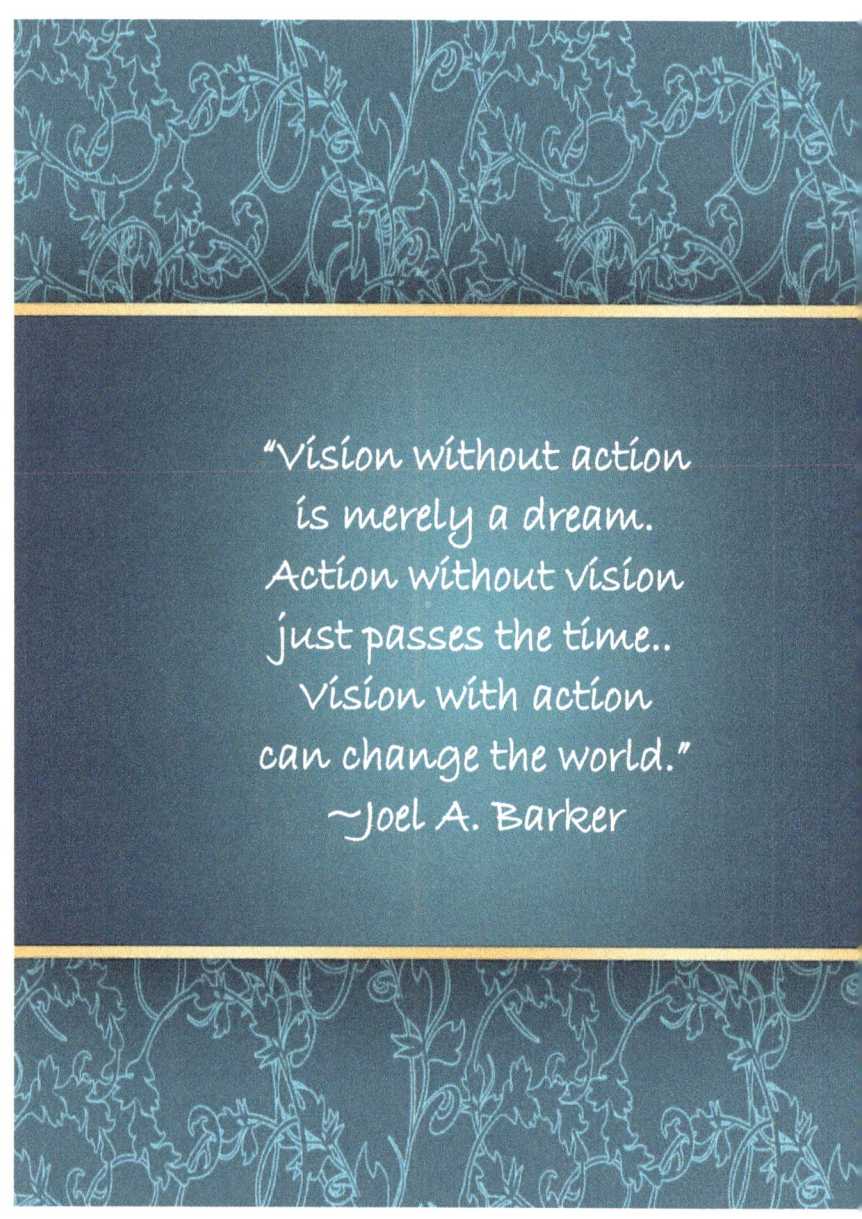

"Vision without action
is merely a dream.
Action without vision
just passes the time..
Vision with action
can change the world."
~Joel A. Barker

Mission-Minded

With the ever-evolving world and competing priorities that consume your time and attention, staying focused on your financial goals can be challenging. Creating a personal financial mission statement can help you identify your values and goals to help you recognize what is important to you. This mission statement then becomes the guiding light in decisions being made. Because of said mission statement, there will be a clear delineation indicating if your decision is moving you closer to or further from success.

This statement summarizes your household's objective reason for pursuing financial security in a few impactful sentences. Your household could be just you, you and your spouse, or you and your family. A solid financial mission statement will precisely explain what your household wants to achieve financially and the roadmap to get there.

It took several discussions and a few drafts before my husband and I agreed on a statement. Do not feel pressure to do it in one day. It may take you days, weeks, or even months AND THAT'S OK! The key is being consistent in working on your mission statement.

Here's an example of a financial mission statement:

The financial mission of the Morris household is to gain total financial freedom and be completely liberated from the vicious debt cycle. By not creating new liabilities while we aggressively attack our debt, we will put maximum effort in building our retirement funds so that we can retire at the age of 55, be fully devoted to serving the Church and community, travelling the world, and actively teaching our children about wealth management.

ACTION: Answer the following questions:

What does financial freedom look like for you? When do you hope to achieve it?

_____

_____

_____

_____

_____

If you had an inexhaustible supply of money, what would you do in life?

_____

_____

_____

_____

_____

What are you most passionate about?

_____

_____

_____

_____

_____

What do you hope to achieve in your life, and how will money play a role in getting you there?

_____

_____

_____

_____

_____

What does a financially secure future look like to you?

_____

_____

_____

_____

_____

Why is teaching your children about debt important to you?

_____

_____

_____

_____

_____

What type of legacy do you wish to leave?

_____

_____

_____

_____

_____

What are your most important saving goals today?

_____

_____

_____

_____

_____

Considering the above questions, write your personal financial mission statement.

_____

_____

_____

_____

_____

_____

TIPS

- Determine the problem or opportunities you want to address in your mission statement
- Remember, when drafting your mission statement, money should not be the end goal. Instead, view money as a tool to help facilitate meeting a goal.

RECOMMENDATIONS

Websites

- [The Five-Step Plan for Creating Personal Mission Statements](#)
- [Using a Financial Purpose Statement](#)

"Courage isn't having the strength to go on – it is going on when you don't have the strength."

~Napoleon Bonaparte

From Goals to Greatness

Identifying your goals is the first step toward making them a reality. Whether it's paying off a credit card, getting out of debt, or saving for an important purchase, decide on the financial goal that's most important to you. In planning your goals, keep the SMART method in mind.

Plan to work, then work the plan. It's as easy as 1, 2, 3.

1. List your goal. Make it real by adding monetary value to the goal.
2. Create a plan **and** timetable that will move you towards the goal.
3. WORK THE PLAN!

Monitor your progress and adjust any portion of the SMART steps, as necessary.

ACTION: List your financial goals.

Financial Goal	Short-, Mid-, Long-Term	Estimated Cost	Time of Completion	Level of Priority

*Short-term (1-12 months); mid-term (1-3 years); and long term (more than three years).
**Level of priority: Essential, Unessential but important, and Indulgent want.

Go to www.21DaySpendingDetox.com to download the workshee

Goal Check-In

*Do a **quarterly goal check-in** to see how you are progressing and if any adjustments are required.*

Are modifications required for your goals? If so, which one(s)? What are the needed changes? What's your new end date? How does this impact your goal?

_____

_____

_____

_____

_____

_____

_____

_____

Conduct a year-end review

What has changed for you? With you? For your household? For your marriage?

_____

_____

_____

_____

_____

_____

_____

_____

What has remained the same?

_____

_____

_____

_____

_____

_____

_____

List your top 3 goals you've accomplished.

1._____

_____

2._____

_____

3._____

_____

List your top 3 goals that are still progressing.

1._____

_____

2._____

_____

3._____

_____

List your top 3 goals which need to change?

1._____

_____

2._____

_____

3._____

_____

How much have you saved?

_____

How much went towards retirement?

_____

How much did you invest?

_____

What were the returns on your investments?

_____

_____

List 3 stocks/investments you will make next year.

1._____
2._____
3._____

How much did you invest in expanding your knowledge and skillset? What was the investment?

_____

How much has your debt decreased?

_____

Have you accumulated any new debt? If so, was / were the debt(s) need-based or want-based?

_____

_____

_____

_____

How much has your income increased?

_____

How much did you contribute towards your children's college fund?

_____

How much did you give to charitable organizations?

_____

TIPS

- Your goals shouldn't be dependent on other people or contingent upon external factors you can't control.
- Write down your goals and put them in a place where you can see them daily.
- For each goal, list the steps you believe it would take to accomplish them.
- List potential risks to accomplishing your goals and begin to think of ways to mitigate said risks.

RECOMMENDED RESOURCES

Website

- Personal Goal Setting

Books

- Creating Your Best Life by Caroline Adams Miller
- Goals: How to Get the Most out of Your Life by Zig Ziglar
- How to Win Friends and Influence People by Dale Carnegie

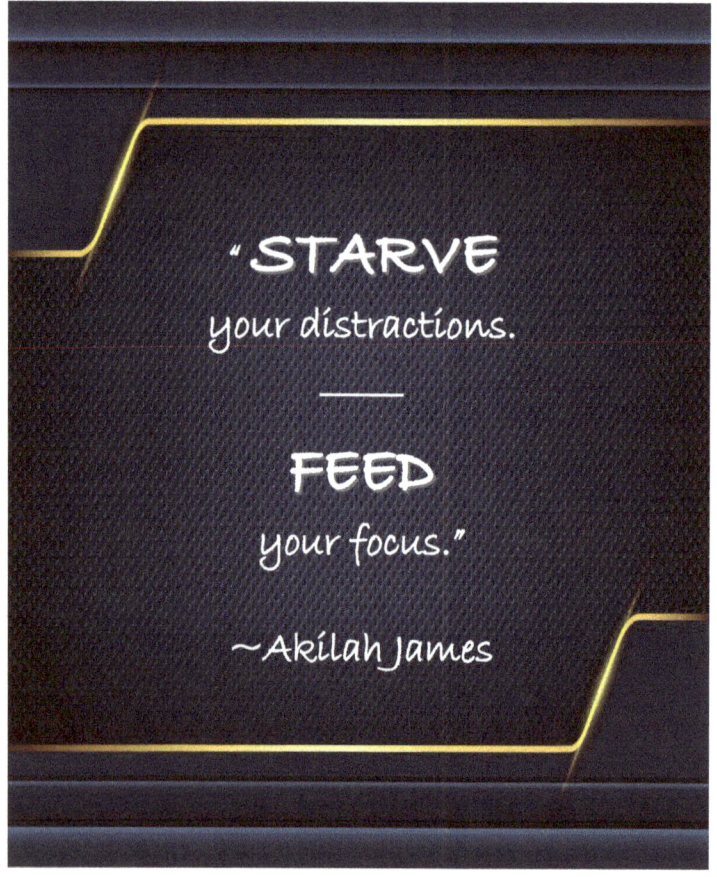

Friends...How Many of Us Have Them?

Part of your genetic makeup desires connection, no matter if you identify as an introvert or extrovert. Relationships help make the human experience more palatable, especially when it comes to slaying giants, crushing goals, and succeeding in this game called life! An accountability partner is one such relationship that could be the missing link to your success.

The right person holding you up and helping you be accountable can be the morale boost that pushes you over the top. Your partner should be there to remind you of the person you are striving to be. A prime partner will not only *call you out* on your sin, but also *call you up* to the person you want to become.

Some have said "I hold myself accountable, so I don't need another person doing what I'm already doing." Taking ownership and self-check ins are great but will you be disciplined enough to stay the course? Will you hold yourself accountable for not accomplishing all your tasks for the week? Will you ask yourself the tough questions and then seek to understand why you do what you do?

Although self-accountability is great, having an external perspective using a different lens will shed a varying light on the situation. Your ally will be there to challenge you to change when you may let yourself off easy. They will not tolerate the excuses of procrastination and self-pity. They will empathize with you while still holding you responsible for doing the work.

ACTION: Create a list of potential individuals you trust and share with them your intentions to connect with an accountability partner. The list should include individuals you hold in high regard.

_____   _____

_____   _____

_____   _____

_____   _____

_____   _____

Some questions to ask your potential accountability partner during the vetting process (yes, you should interview them to gain insight on their experiences and skillset) can be:

1. Do you have the time to devote to this partnership?
2. How do you manage competing priorities?
3. How have you established work-life balance?
4. How often do you meet with _your_ accountability partner?
5. What skills do you have to contribute to holding someone accountable?
6. What is your communication style?
7. How do you think you'll benefit from this partnership?
8. What are some of your strongest personality traits?
9. What strategies do you use to meet your goals?
10. How do you overcome obstacles, prevent procrastination, and deal with distractions?

Once you find a probable candidate, schedule the first four meetings, which should cover the following:

Meeting 1: RULES OF ENGAGEMENT

- Agree on day, time, frequency, types of communication, and discuss behavioral tendencies.

Frequency	Day	Time 30-60 min	Form of Communication	Follow-Up Communication
Daily	Monday		In-Person	Email
___Days Per Week	Tuesday		Video Conference	Text
Weekly	Wednesday		Telephone	
Bi-Weekly	Thursday			
Monthly	Friday			
	Saturday			
	Sunday			

	Challenge	Accountability Partner Responsibility
T E N D E N C I E S	I make excuses and go easy on myself	Will call me out and give me tough love
	I get overwhelmed	Helps me to prioritize and find work-life balance
	I'm motivated by competition	Helps me to focus on my goals and not be consumed with others' progress
	I hate competition	Ensures that I am not operating in fear and I am bringing my best to the table
	Positivity inspires me	Balances positive reinforcement while speaking the truth of needful changes
	I have trouble saying no	Will help me set and enforce boundaries
	I procrastinate	Will help me prioritize and have consistency

Go to www.21DaySpendingDetox.com to download a copy of the spreadsheets.

- Come to a mutual understanding that this constitutes a trial period for the partnership and that either person can gracefully withdraw from the partnership with no hard feelings.
- Share your overall vision, goals, and needs for the partnership.
- Prepare for the next meeting by discussing the assignment, *Goals and Gaps*
  1. List the goals you want to accomplish. This will become your roadmap for the partnership.
  2. Rate where you believe you are in achieving them
     5 = nearly no gap between where I am and where I **WANT** to be (95%+ achieved)
     4 = minor gap (80% achieved)
     3 = moderate gap (70% achieved)
     2 = meaningful gap (40% achieved)
     1 = major gap (10% or less achieved)

Meeting 2: GOALS AND GAPS

- Present your goals and gaps.
- Discuss why these are your goals as well as why you assigned the ratings to each of the respective goals.
- Select one of your smallest gaps to address. You are starting small to get quick wins to gather momentum and motivation.
- Your assignment for the next session is to list milestones to help achieve that goal.

Meeting 3: PLAN ON A PAGE

- Share your goal and the corresponding milestones it will take to achieve it.
- The Accountability Partner will provide feedback on the milestones.
  - Are they specific?
  - Are they measurable?
  - Are they challenging?
  - Are they achievable?
  - Is the timeframe realistic?
- Together, make an action plan to execute each milestone.

Meeting 4: ASSESS AND ACCELERATE

- Discuss your progress.
- Talk about any distractions or things that would derail milestone achievement.
- Look for ways to mitigate those risks.
- Discuss the partnership's progress and decide if it will continue. If so, proceed with the established meeting schedule.

TIPS

- Set a start AND end time for each meeting.
- Make recurring meetings so that you can add them to your calendars as a standing meeting.
- If you are unable to meet, reschedule within the same day you notify your partner.
- Establish goals and put a time limit on them. It's ok to have grand goals but ensure you have the tasks and steps that will help you tackle it one milestone at a time.

- Before leaving each meeting, identify the action items for each person to do before the next meeting.
- Each meeting should include a review of goal-related progress and feedback, along with a follow-up email/text message of the agreed upon next steps/actions/milestones that are to be done between accountability sessions.
- Choose one thing to work on at a time. It may be tempting to tackle multiple goals at once but that's a sneaky and subtle way to sabotage your success.
- Have a check-in after the first month to ensure the partnership is giving what it needs. There is no harm in adjusting as needed and even ending the partnership if it is not serving the intended purpose.
- Find someone who is trustworthy. Remember, you will become vulnerable and transparent in this process, so you'll need a non-judgmental partner who will protect your privacy.
- Find a partner who is disciplined. There are times when you need to be pushed past procrastination or just need some motivation. They can pull you out of your stress and bring you back on the right path with a discussion and some inspiration.
- Find someone who will not allow you to be comfortable with mediocrity. They drive you to be your best, authentic self. They will challenge you to work harder when you start to relax or fall behind.
- Find someone who is a great communicator, as this role is essential in providing honest feedback. They must know how to tactfully provide constructive criticism and build the person up at the same time!

- Find someone who is equally passionate and committed to change.
- Work on being an active listener. Do not listen to respond, but listen to hear and understand, then provide feedback.
- If you find a session turning into a time of complaining and blaming, lovingly yet firmly redirect the conversation to focus on a solution.
- Exclude your close friends and spouses when considering an accountability partner; this will help to preserve the relationship when they need to call you out on your crap or so the partnership does not turn into a 'shooting the breeze' session. Every moment must be deliberate and intentional. The essence of the relationship is to provide honest feedback and not to waste time.

RECOMMENDED RESOURCES

Apps

- Supporti
- Momentum Buddy

"An accountability partner is able to perceive what you can't see when blind spots and weaknesses block your vision."

– Charles Stanley

Budget Battles

If your goal is to obtain financial freedom, conquering the battle of the budget is paramount, as it is the foundation to every successful financial strategy. Whether you're a thousandaire or a billionaire, *you need to know where your money is going.*

Of next importance is how you view budgeting. A budget is there to help provide freedom not restrictions. With an effective budget, you have a clear view of where every penny is allocated and how you can freely maneuver within those parameters.

A negative mindset and unclear purpose can lead to abandonment of your money mission. With many roads leading to indulgence but masked as self-care, having the proper tools, people, and words in place can help you stay on the right track. Constant reminders of your financial goals help to ward off depreciating willpower to say "no" to destructive financial habits.

REPEAT AFTER ME:

- I make a conscious decision to spend money wisely.
- My goals will become a reality because I put the work in and carefully budget.
- I am disciplined to make difficult financial decisions.
- I am ok with setting boundaries and telling people NO.
- I spend money on what matters to me and not to the Joneses.

ACTION: Complete the monthly budget worksheet.

MONTHLY BUDGET

SUMMARY	
Category	Amount
Income	0.00
Expenses	0.00
Savings	0.00

Month
Year

SOURCES OF INCOME	
Category	Amount
Salary / wages after taxes	
Tips, Bonus, Side Job	
Spouse's salary after taxes	
Child Support	
Alimony	
Rental Income	
Capital Gains Income	
Profit from sales of products and services	
Interest Income	
Dividend Income	
Royalty & Licensing Income	
Advertising Income	
Refunds / Reimbursements	
Gifts Received	
Other	
TOTAL INCOME	0.00

SAVINGS			
Category	Budget	Actual	Difference
Emergency Funds			
Retirement			
Investments			
Child Education			
Holidays			
Travel			
Repairs / Renovations			
General Savings Account			
Other			
TOTAL SAVINGS	0	0	

EXPENSES

HOUSING	Budget	Actual	Difference
Mortgage / Rent			
2nd Mortgage			
HELOC			
Home Owner / Rental Insurance			
Home Insurance			
HOA / Condo Fees			
Maintenance Fees			
Lawn / Garden Maintenance			
Repairs			
Other			
Other			
Other			
TOTAL HOUSING EXPENSES	$ -	$ -	$ -

DEBTS	Budget	Actual	Difference
Student Loan			
Spouse Student Loan			
Personal Loan			
Business Loan			
Line of Credit			
Consolidation Loan			
Credit Cards			
Pay in 4 Loan (Klarna, AfterPay, Affirm, etc)			
Taxes			
Alimony			
Child Support			
Other			
TOTAL DEBTS	0.00	0.00	

UTILITIES	Budget	Actual	Difference
Gas			
Electricity			
Water			
Sewer			
Garbage / Trash			
Telephone			
Cell Phone			
Internet			
Cable			
Alarm System			
Other			
TOTAL UTILITIES EXPENSES	0.00	0.00	0.00

AUXILLARY ACTIVITIES	Budget	Actual	Difference
Membership Dues			
Movies			
Gym			
Sports			
Lottery / Gambling			
Dining Out			
Concert			
Bowling			
Smoking			
Drinking			
Other			
TOTAL AUXILLARY ACTIVITIES	0.00	0.00	

TRANSPORTATION	Budget	Actual	Difference
Vehicle #1 Payment			
Vehicle #2 Payment			
Motorcycle Payment			
Auto Insurance			
Motorcycle Insurance			
Gas			
Maintenance			
Repairs			
Bus Pass			
Train Fare			
Taxi / Uber			
Toll Fees			
Parking Fees			
License / Registration Fees			
Smog / Air Quality Test			
Vehicle Repairs			
Other			
TOTAL TRANSPORTATION EXPENSES	0.00	0.00	0.00

DAILY LIVING	Budget	Actual	Difference
Child Care			
K-12 Education			
Adult Education			
Life/Funeral Insurance			
Health Insurance			
Dr. Co-Payment			
Medicine / Prescriptions / Supplements			
Pet Insurance			
Pet Food			
Pet Maintenance			
Salon / Barber			
Groceries			
Personal Care			
Clothing / Shoes			
Massage			
Dry Cleaning / Laundromat			
Other			
TOTAL DAILY LIVING	0.00	0.00	

Subscriptions	Budget	Actual	Difference
Legal Services (LegalZoom, RocketLawyer, etc)			
Food Services (GrubHub, UberEats, etc.)			
Streaming Services (Disney+, Hulu, etc.)			
Podcasts, Social Media (Patreon, etc.)			
Business Services (Postage, eCloud storage, etc.)			
Fitness Apps			
Clothing and Shoes			
Gaming Services			
Magazines			
Books			
Business Journals			
Other			
Other			
Other			
Other			
TOTAL SUBSCRIPTION EXPENSES	0.00	0.00	0.00

CHARITY / DONATIONS	Budget	Actual	Difference
Religious Giving / Tithes / Offerings			
Charitable Contributions			
Gifts Given			
Other			
Other			
TOTAL CHARITY	0.00	0.00	

Notes:

Go to www.21DaySpendingDetox.com to download a copy of the Budget spreadsheet.

TIPS

- Review your budget monthly and adjust as necessary. Monthly needs may fluctuate depending on seasons and life celebrations.
- If you've allocated funds to go out, leave your credit cards at home, withdraw that specified cash amount from your account, and keep all receipts to compare what you allocated to what you actually spent. It's all about holding yourself accountable.
- If using the envelope system, do not borrow from one envelope to cover expenses for another category.

RECOMMENDED RESOURCES

Books

- [Total Money Makeover](#) by Dave Ramsey
- [Get Good with Money](#) by Tiffany "The Budgetnista" Aliche

Apps

- [Rocket Money](#) (formerly True Bill)
- [Ramsey+](#)
- [Acorn](#)
- [Honeydue](#) (for couples)

"You've got to get up every morning
with determination
if you're going to go to bed
with satisfaction."
~ George Lorimer

Planning for Power

As a Strategic Sourcing person by trade, one of the things I do in preparation for major negotiations is to create a negotiation grid of the things I am looking to accomplish. I call it 'planning for power.' The more armed I am with a detailed plan, the more likely I will be successful in getting what I want. And so it goes with financial planning.

Financial planning is the process of taking a comprehensive look at your financial situation and building a specific plan that helps facilitate reaching your goals.

A major component in curating a strategic plan is being armed with knowledge. Before you can put a plan in place, you must first know what's coming out (liabilities / debts) and going in (sources of income and assets).

ACTION: Complete the Financial Plan worksheet.

Go to www.21DaySpendingDetox.com to download the worksheet.

Goals	List debt goals	
	List savings goals	
	List investment goals	
	List retirement savings goals	
	List retirement lifestyle goals	
	List vacation goals	
	List education goals	
	List business goals	
Budgeting	List Assets	
	List Income	
	List Expenses	
	List Debt	
	List Savings	
Investments	List investment accounts and balances	
	Attach investment portfolio return report	
	List asset allocation plans	
Retirement	Retirement income estimates from 401k	
	Retirement income estimates from IRA	
	Retirement income estimates from pension	
Estate Planning	List estate / inheritance tax estimates	
	Attach copy of signed and notarized living will	
Taxes	List contribution towards income tax	
	List contributions towards IRA and 401k	
	List estimated taxes on capital gains	
Insurance and Risk Management	List your insurance policiies, amounts and beneficiaries	
	List your annuities and amounts	

TIPS

- Calculate your net worth by subtracting your assets from your liabilities. Assets include your home, car, or a piece of art, and also includes bank accounts, insurance policies, and investments. A list of liabilities can include loans, mortgages, rent, and other bills.
- Use the budget worksheet on page 56 to get a comprehensive breakdown of your income and expenses.
- Get aggressive with attacking your debt. By eliminating it, you free up more capital to invest and save.
- To reduce or altogether eliminate the negative impact of a tax bill for the coming year, allocate a fixed amount of income towards taxes you could potentially owe.

RECOMMENDED RESOURCES

Books

- [I Am Net Worthy](#) by Chris Smith
- [The Million-Dollar Financial Advisor](#) by David J. Mullen Jr.

A seedling Chinese Bamboo Tree requires water, sunshine, good soil, and consistent care. But even all the consistent, intentional, and proper care, nothing will sprout
for the first year.
Or the second year.
Or the third year.
But if you keep watering and caring for that seed, in the fifth year, the tree will sprout. and when it does, it can grow 80ft in just 6 weeks!
DON'T GIVE UP!
You may be days or hours from a major sprouting.

Purpose, Path, Plan, and Process

Obstacles. Detours. Roadblocks. Setbacks. Denials.
None of these are welcomed as you traverse life's path, yet they may very well be a part of your process. From sports to medicine and all ranges of the life spectrum in between, people have been inundated with the overutilized yet undervalued catchphrase, 'trust the process.'

Learning to allow the process to work itself in and through you will help you to simply 'let it go' and relinquish obsessive control of every micrometer of your plan.
Even when things don't go your way, allowing the process to be what it is frees you from the inclination to help (desperately working to solve everything) or hide (crawl under a rock and completely ignore the situation as if it didn't exist). Both are hindrances to progress, as they show a lack of faith and fortitude in knowing that things will eventually work out in its own time.

Trusting the process undoubtedly knows that where you are now will not be your final resting place. No matter how bleak and bad, it won't always be like that.

ACTION: Answer the following questions.

In what area(s) of your life do you currently exert the most control? How and why?

_____
_____
_____
_____
_____
_____

What do you believe is the payoff (emotionally, financially, professionally, etc.) to exerting control in this way? What does this allow you to feel or avoid feeling?

_____
_____
_____
_____
_____
_____

How might your life (or others' lives) be impacted if you let go of control in this area of your life?

_____
_____
_____
_____
_____
_____

What's one thing you can do differently today to let go of control in this area of your life?

_____

_____

_____

_____

_____

_____

What's something you can tell yourself if/when you're struggling with letting go?

_____

_____

_____

_____

_____

_____

TIP

- Don't rush through the process that you end up missing the opportunity to learn and grow.

RECOMMENDED RESOURCES

Book

- [Discover Your Purpose](#) by Rhys Thomas

Website

- [Start Finding Your Purpose and Unlock Your Best Life](#)

"Consistency transforms average into excellence."
~Unknown

Debt Free Is for Me!

Paying off debt can seem overwhelming, but the way you attack that elephant of debt is one step at a time. Start by listing each of your debts. This very act can feel intimidating, but I promise, once you have everything listed and have a clear view of what you really owe, it will make a major difference in developing a strategy to eliminate debt and then executing said strategy.

ACTION: List each of your debts.

DATE	DEBT	STARTING BALANCE	CURRENT BALANCE	INTEREST	MONTHLY PAYMENT

Go to www.21DaySpendingDetox.com to download the worksheet.

After you have ALL your debt listed, determine how you want to tackle the debt. There are four main strategies for paying off debt: the Snowball Method, the Largest Balance, Highest Interest Rate, and Consolidation.

Strategy	How It Works	Next steps
Snowball Method	1. Start with the paying the smallest debt as quickly as possible 2. Continue making minimum payments on all other debt	Once the smallest debt is paid off, take the money you would have used for that debt and now apply it to the next smallest debt.
Largest Balance	1. Start by paying the debt with the largest balance as quickly as possible. 2. Continue making minimum payments on all other debt	Once the largest balance debt is paid off, take the money you would have used for that debt and now apply it to the next largest debt.
Highest Interest Rate	1. Start by paying the debt with the highest interest rate. 2. Continue making minimum payments on all other debt.	Once the highest interest debt is paid off, take the money you would have used for that debt and now apply it to the next highest interest debt.
Debt Consolidation	Combine all debts into one account, so that you're only making one monthly payment on all your debt	Avoid creating any new debt until the consolidation is paid in full.

TIPS

- When making an extra payment in the same month, ensure that it goes to the principal, if applicable.
  - Check with your lender to ensure there's no fee for prepayments.
- If you find that you are still barely above water, consider debt consolidation/debt management.

  - This allows you to make a single monthly payment on all your unsecured debts (i.e. personal loans, credit cards, medical bills — mostly all bills outside of mortgage, federal student loans, and auto loans) month to a credit counseling agency, which distributes it among your creditors until the plan is paid in full.
  - Interest rates are reduced, and fees may be waived, however your credit card accounts will be closed while you are on the plan.
- Don't borrow against the equity in your home, as it puts your home at risk of foreclosure, and you may be turning unsecured debt that could be wiped out in bankruptcy into secured debt that can't be.
- Try to avoid borrowing money from workplace retirement accounts. If you lose your job, the loans can become inadvertent withdrawals and trigger a tax bill.

RECOMMENDED RESOURCES

Websites

- National Foundation for Credit Counseling
- Financial Counseling Association of America

"Compound interest is the 8th

wonder of the world. He who

understands it, earns it.

He who doesn't, pays it."

~Albert Einstein

Scoring to New Heights

Never has a number caused more panic or praise, fear or freedom, anxiety or acceptance than that three-digit credit score. While on your journey to financial independence, you may find it necessary to make major purchases that are credit-score dependent. Your score not only determines *if* you qualify for financing but also your interest rate. Bottom line, it affects your quality of life (because who wants to pay 29.4% interest).

Understanding what range of the spectrum your credit score lands will determine the level of effort needed to help improve it.

ACTION: List your credit score from all **SIX** credit agencies/bureaus.

Bureau	Score	Date
Experian		
Eqifax		
Transunion		
Innovis		
PRBC		
SageStream		
Advanced Resolution Service		

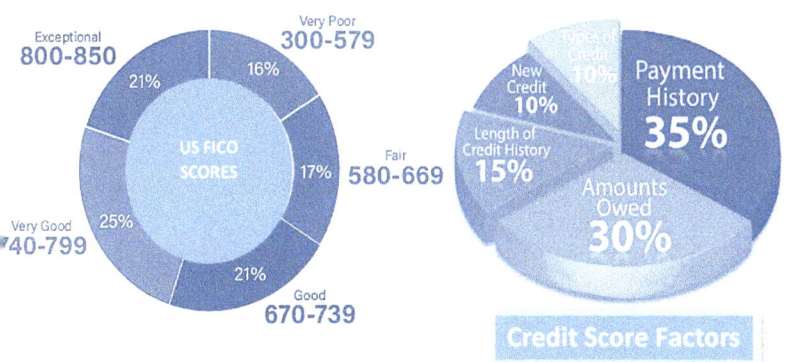

TIPS

- If you have a loved one or someone you trust with a good credit score, they can add you as an authorized user to their account. This allows you to make purchases. But the primary account holder is ultimately responsible for payments. And their responsible use can help build your credit and boost your score.

- As you're working your way to better credit, a secured credit card may be helpful. You can make purchases with it, just like a traditional credit card. But it's considered "secured" because it requires you to put money down as a security deposit to open the account.

- When you have a secured card, some credit card companies like Capital One report your status to the credit bureaus. So, if you're paying at least your minimum payment on time and using your card responsibly, it could help you improve your credit.

RECOMMENDED RESOURCES

Websites

- Experian
- Eqifax
- Transunion
- Innovis
- PRBC
- SageStream
- Advanced Resolution Service

"We can have all the knowledge in the world, but it means nothing without the wisdom to know what to do with it."

~C.A. Morris

It's Just Emotions Taking Me Over

With your money mindset being affected by experiences and emotions, it is no surprise that emotions play a major part in your spending. During periods of sadness, stress and even happiness, you may find yourself needlessly spending money.

ACTION: Track your spending and the thoughts you had while purchasing the item(s).

Date	Time	Amount of Purchase	Budgeted Item (Y or N)	Reason for the Purchase	Thoughts & Feelings at Time of Purchase

Go to www.21DaySpendingDetox.com to download the worksheet.

ACTION: Complete the following sentences:

Spending makes me feel...

_____

_____

_____

When I'm angry, I ...

_____

_____

_____

When I'm sad, I ...

_____

_____

_____

When I'm happy, I...

_____

_____

_____

When I can't sleep, I ...

_____

_____

_____

When I'm bored, I …

_____

_____

_____

When I'm hungry, I …

_____

_____

_____

When I'm scared, I …

_____

_____

_____

When I'm anxious, I …

_____

_____

_____

When I celebrate, I …

_____

_____

_____

When I'm lonely, I …

_____

_____

_____

When I'm overlooked, I…

_____

_____

_____

What are your greatest fears about money?

_____

_____

_____

What are your childhood memories of money?

_____

_____

_____

_____

_____

_____

_____

_____

TIPS

- When using the 24 to 48-hour 'wait rule,' where you let your items sit in your online shopping cart for a 'cool-down' period before purchasing,

    1. Use this time to decide how the purchase would impact your budget. Ask yourself if you really need the item — and if it's worth the spend. Determine if It moves you closer towards your goals. Will it impact the quality of your life?

    2. Examine how you felt when you were browsing for said items.

- Remove spending apps from your phone and unsubscribe to emails and text messages encouraging you to spend.

- Review your spending log monthly, adjust as needed, and celebrate your progress, just not with a purchase!

RECOMMENDED RESOURCES

Book

- The Psychology of Money by Morgan Housel

Websites

- [Ways to Control Emotional Spending](#)
- [6 Danger Signs of Emotional Spending](#)
- [The Long History of Retail Therapy](#)

"The ability to discipline
yourself to delay
gratification in the short term
in order to enjoy greater
rewards in the long term is
the indispensable prerequisite
for success."

~Brian Tracy

Spending Spouses

From the societal pressure to keep up with 'The Joneses' and a lack of trust to waning intimacy and depression, the reasons run the gamut of why one spouse may spend money uncontrollably.

Not only is having those difficult money conversations critical to your financial health but equally needed for the health and longevity of your marriage. Talking about your goals and desires will help to create a marriage and money mission statement.

ACTION: Each spouse is to answer the following questions[1]

What is your most painful money memory?

_____

_____

_____

_____

_____

_____

What is your most joyful money memory?

_____

_____

_____

_____

_____

_____

How did these experiences shape your relationship with money?

_____

_____

_____

_____

_____

What are 3 things your parents or family taught you about money?

1._____

_____

2._____

_____

3._____

_____

Which lessons have you applied to your financial life?

_____

_____

_____

_____

_____

Growing up, did you see your family as rich, poor, or middle class? Why?

_____

_____

_____

_____

_____

What were your family's values about money? Are these values applicable for you now?

_____

_____

_____

_____

_____

What is your greatest financial fear?

_____

_____

_____

_____

_____

_____

_____

What are you willing to do differently when it comes to money?

_____

_____

_____

_____

_____

Where do you want to be financially in the next year? 3 years? 5 years? 10 years?

_____

_____

_____

_____

_____

What do you wish I (your spouse) did more of and less of with regards to money?

_____

_____

_____

_____

_____

_____

TIPS

- If talking about money is difficult for you and your spouse, go to a neutrally peaceful place you both enjoy outside of the home.
- Create the household budget and savings plan together so that you can jointly establish what is realistically doable and manage to those expectations.
- Always reinforce your desire to be a strong team in achieving your goals.
- Do not begin by accusing your spouse of wrongdoing or by pointing out faults. Deserved or not, this sort of treatment will only drive a wedge between the two of you and make it harder to communicate. Instead, approach the subject in a loving manner.

RECOMMENDED RESOURCES

- Financially Ever After by Jeff Opdyke
- Smart Couples Finish Rich by David Bach

Before you speak

THINK

T – Is it true?

H – Is it helpful?

I – Is it inspiring?

N – Is it necessary?

K – Is it kind?

~Unknown

Cleared for Takeoff

Home should be your place of peace and comfort, but when home is chaotic and cluttered, you may seek other ways to bring you comfort. A cluttered kitchen, for example, encourages you to order takeout or dine out as opposed to having a clean and organized kitchen, which promotes meal prep and cooking.

A cluttered environment lends itself to a propensity to procrastinate, feeling dissatisfied as a whole, and a diminished wherewithal to concentrate. With these feelings and behaviors in tow, it weighs down on your ability to make wise financial decisions.

All your accumulated possessions, both mentally and physically, occupy space. While the physicality invades your immediate surroundings, mental clutter lessens your short-term memory and affects your efficiency in processing information. Instead of doing your budget, researching stocks, or reviewing your retirement plan, clutter subconsciously plants you deeper into the comfortability of complacency, where you avoid the task at hand. You end up binge watching a 10-part series on TV instead of working on the needful.

Financial clutter can block your progress toward a clear financial path and will end up costing you in the long run. From unpaid bills (because you've allowed the mail and email to pile up) to duplicate purchases, clutter's slow leak can cause you to fall flat in achieving your financial goals.

I challenge you to approach your clutter head-on. Don't wait until you feel overwhelmed to get a handle on your clutter. A total transformation will not happen instantly—take things slow to avoid burnout, so start with small goals.

ACTION: Create a list of spaces that you will declutter and organize.

_____	_____
_____	_____
_____	_____
_____	_____
_____	_____
_____	_____

Some areas to consider purging and organizing:

1. Kitchen pantry
2. Clothes closet
3. Mail pile
4. Fridge
5. Freezer
6. Junk drawer
7. CD and DVD collection
8. Linen closet
9. Medicine cabinet
10. Bathroom cabinet
11. Tupperware cabinet
12. Laundry room
13. Garage
14. Nightstand
15. Silverware drawer
16. Spices cabinet
17. Cleaning supplies cabinet
18. Bookshelf
19. Purses and accessories
20. Kids' toys
21. Kids' closet and drawers

TIPS

- Start with a small space, like a 'junk drawer,' then move to bigger spaces and projects. Do your work in 30-minute increments to avoid feeling overwhelmed.
- Make decluttering part of your weekly routine. If you typically do a thorough house cleaning once a week or biweekly, take 15 to 30 minutes to go through your spaces prone to clutter (closet, pantry, 'junk drawers.') You can put your closet back in order by picking clothing up from the floor, hanging up your dry cleaning the day you pick it up, putting away laundry the day you wash it, and putting away shoes and other accessories the day you wear it.
- Institute a one-in-one-out system. If you buy an item, you must put one item in the bag to donate. This system helps to keep clutter at bay. At the very least, you will be in a steady state of maintenance after you've done the big purge.

Below are some ways in which you can remove mental clutter in an attempt to improve your overall well-being:

- Do a digital detox: Give your mind and eyes a break by fasting from social media; go to your settings and turn off all phone notifications, remove any unused apps on your mobile devices, and reduce and restrict screen time on all electronic devices (including television).
- Keep a strong support system: Your friends and family who support you are important so keep them close and rely on them. If you have people in your life who exhibit negative energy or who bring you down, then it is time to get rid of them. Toxic

relationships are one of the biggest dictators of mental clutter.

- Adopt healthy lifestyle decisions: Exercise daily, avoid sugary and processed snacks, drink lots of water, limit alcohol and caffeine, and adopt a healthy sleep routine.

RECOMMENDED RESOURCES

Apps

- Toss – This app helps you declutter fast and easy, one day at a time by assigning daily tasks to complete, with most tasks only requiring minutes of your time.
- Get Rid of It – This app helps you become a minimalist by getting rid of items that has no value in your life. This 30-day challenge will help you purge your space as well as provide tips on maintaining a decluttered lifestyle (only on Android devices).
- Tody – This is a cleaning management app that assist you with scheduling and tracking your cleaning projects. Tasks are ranked by greatest importance; you can monitor the areas requiring the most attention, and you can assign tasks to others in your household.
- Decluttr – For those with a lot of clothes, books, games, CDs, DVDs, and other tech items to declutter, you can sell them with this free app. Also check out OfferUp, LetGo, Poshmark, Vestiaire, Gazelle, eBay and Craigslist.
- Centriq – This app is designed to help declutter papers (manuals, catalogs, registrations, warranties, etc.) related to appliances, equipment,

tools, and other household electronics. It not only catalogs your documents, but it also checks national databases for product safety and recalls.

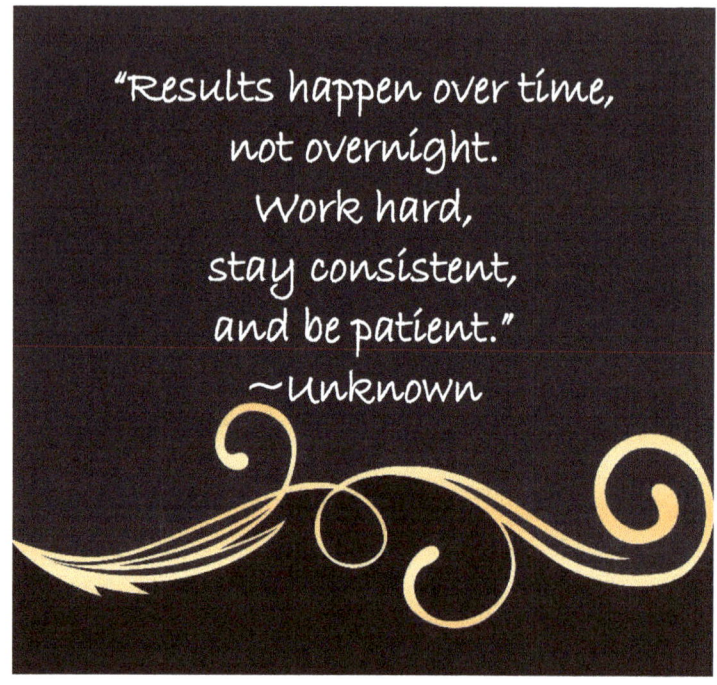

"Results happen over time,
not overnight.
Work hard,
stay consistent,
and be patient."
~Unknown

Free Flow of Funds

Growing your net worth? Getting out of debt? Growing your emergency fund? Diversifying your retirement savings? Taking your dream vacation across the Mediterranean? No matter the reason of wanting more money, multiple streams of income is rapidly becoming the method in which people are employing to augment their salary. The additional stream may not necessarily bring in what your traditional job does, yet, if worked properly, it could undoubtedly aid in meeting your financial goals.

Given you only have 1440 minutes per day, working multiple traditional jobs will shorten your free time. Aside from asking for a raise, begin to think how you can creatively increase your income with minimal impact on your time. Some examples are:

- Real estate / rental property
- Invest
- Create an online store (Etsy) for your hobby
- Sell products on an Amazon/eBay ecommerce store
- Write an e-book
- Write a blog and monetize it with ads
- Become a rideshare driver (Uber, Lyft)
- Rent your house / room through Air BnB
- Create an online course from your expertise
- Create a consulting company from your experience, education, and expertise
- Develop social media content (YouTube videos sell well)

ACTION: Name 5 things you can do right now to help generate additional income.

1._____

_____

_____

2._____

_____

_____

3._____

_____

_____

4._____

_____

_____

5._____

_____

_____

TIPS

- Join the sharing economy. In addition to Airbnb, you can rent out your car on Turo, rent out your camera equipment on KitSplit, rent your snowboard or bike on Spinlister, or rent your sailboat on Sailo.
- When assessing how you can generate multiple income streams, consider these factors:
  - *Saving Time*: The ideal source of extra income will allow you to call the shots when it comes to your time. Many people create income streams by working part time as an employee of a company. However, you'll have a lot more flexibility and independence by working for yourself.
  - *Sustainable*: The ideal extra income source will continue to generate cash even when you're not working at it. The idea is to build something that can eventually function without you.
  - *Satisfying*: Generating additional sources of income is a lot of work, so you might as well enjoy what you're doing.

RECOMMEND RESOURCES

Websites and APPS

- Realty Mogul (real estate investment)
- Fundrise (crowdfunding real estate)

- [Robinhood](#) (purchase small amounts of stock at a time)

"To achieve what 1% of the world's population has (Financial Freedom), you must be willing to do what only 1% dare to do... hard work and perseverance of the highest order."
~ Manoj Arora

The Sense and Centsability of Saving

Having exhausted all possibilities but are still struggling to see significant savings, consider accelerating your results by reducing your expenses. Look for 'low-hanging fruit' like dining out, shopping (clothes, shoes, etc.), and entertainment (golf, movies, etc.); these and other items alike can either be eliminated or reduced. Become more streamlined with recurring bills and services like your cell phone bill, cable, internet, etc. Revisit your insurance policies, as your car, health and life insurances can be modified to be more economical. Additionally, save green by going green! Simple acts from commuting and changing light bulbs to closing your curtains help conserve energy and preserve your bank account!

ACTION: Make a list of your subscriptions (Netflix, Hulu, Disney+, etc.) and determine if they can be cancelled.

Subscription	Amount	Frequency of Use	Cancel?

Go to www.21DaySpendingDetox.com to download a copy of the spreadsheet.

TIPS

- Ask for a discount!
- Check for promo codes with online shopping.
- Turn off lights and ceiling fans when not in use.
- Use resources, such as MeetUp and other local community event listings, to find free or low-cost entertainment.
- If possible, avoid rush hour traffic. The constant starting and stopping wreaks havoc on your gas.
- Ensure your hot water heater is set between 120 and 140°F. For every 10-degree reduction in temperature, you can save up to five percent on water heating costs.
- Close your curtains at dusk to stop heat escaping through the windows.

RECOMMENDED RESOURCES

APPs and Websites

- Honey and Rakuten. These browser plug-ins scour the web for the most advantageous discount codes to apply to your online purchase.
- SmartyPig. This is an online savings account for specific goals or purchases. You set a goal and choose the amount you want to contribute each month to reach that goal, and SmartyPig automatically pulls that amount from your checking account each month. You can make your goals public to friends and family, so they can contribute to your goal if they want to.

- GasBuddy. Gas is getting ridiculously expensive so here's a way to save money by comparing prices for gas stations in your area.
- BillShrink. Get a list of cell phone plans or credit cards that are better than what you have. From a short assessment of your current plan and bills, BillShrink will pair you with the most advantageous plan and credit cards that match your needs.
- MoneyAisle. This app helps you locate the highest savings or CD interest rate by allowing banks to bid on the interest rate they're willing to pay you.

"If you can't fly,
then run.
If you can't run,
then walk.
If you can't walk
then crawl.
But whatever you do,
keep moving forward."
~Dr. Marth Luther King Jr.

GOD and Grace

The ebbs and flows of your voyage to financial freedom can bring unpredictable challenges, so it's going to take commitment and faith to stay the course. This faith is not solely in your capability to succeed but in God's ability to mature you through your process, for it's never just about the destination but more about the character that God desires to develop in you. Talking to God (which is the simplistic premise of prayer) about everything, including finances, is an invitation to include Him in all aspects of your life. Inviting God into your finances is something you must do continuously. Whether you are facing financial stresses or financial abundance, prayer should always be an important part of your money journey. It's beyond praying about getting money, beyond tithing and offerings. Ask Him about your financial habits; ask Him to show you what you are not seeing. Ask Him to help you with planning and budgeting. Ask Him to show you your attitude towards money. This is critical if you plan to be the wise steward of what He has entrusted to you.

ACTION: Name 3 areas where you can trust God more.

1._____

_____

_____

2._____

_____

_____

3._____

_____

_____

TIPS

- Ask God to help you shift your focus from the job being THE source to it now being A resource. There are several examples which show how God was the person's needed source: He sent ravens to sustain Elijah (1 Kings 17), Peter found money in a fish to pay taxes (Matthew 17), Peter's large catch of fish (John 21). He has millions of other ways to sustain and get you what you need.

  Your job is not there to meet your needs; that's God's job. He is your ONLY source. Everything else, INCLUDING YOUR JOB, is a resource. Bold statement, I know, yet it does not change the accuracy of it. If your job is your only source, what will you do if something happens to end your tenure there? All I'm saying is take the limits off God to meet your need only through the job. Don't be so consumed and connected to that job that you are unable to pivot and shift if something happens to the job.

- With God being your source, shift your mindset to now see your job as a means of releasing and sharing your gifts, talents, and knowledge with others.

RECOMMENDED RESOURCES

Websites

- Seedtime
- Sound Mind Investing

"Treat your finances as a resource God has provided to fulfill your vision, not a tool to fill your life with luxuries."

~Dr. Myles Munroe

Leftovers and Lists are Life

Most of us can comfortably say that we are blessed to have a broad selection of food to eat at home. This, however, does not give you a license to be wasteful and careless with how you manage it. Just as there is intentionality with saving, investing, and budgeting, you need to keep that same energy when it comes to maintaining your fridge and pantry. This not only goes for minimizing waste by eating leftovers but also monitoring what you have and creating lists prior to going grocery shopping so that you are not buying the same thing three times!

ACTION: Meal plan for the week by listing what you will cook daily. Then based on that, take inventory of your fridge and pantry to determine what you will need to purchase from the store.

Day of the Week	Meal	Grocery List of Items Needed

Go to www.21DaySpendingDetox.com to download a copy of the spreadsheet.

TIPS

- Store smartly. Use glass containers. They allow a side view of what's inside.
- Do a monthly purge on your fridge, freezer, pantry, and cupboards. Use what you have before buying more.
- Eat before you shop; it keeps you from buying based on your immediate need of hunger!
- Buy less packaged convenience foods and do the work yourself (shred your own lettuce and cheese, make your own trail mix).
- Organize your food storage areas to avoid duplicate purchases of the same item.
- Shop with a calculator and tabulate as you shop.
- Bulk-buy your proteins and butcher them at home (i.e., buy a whole chicken and cut it into individual pieces) For my vegetarians and vegans, you can buy your proteins (beans, grains, and tofu) in bulk.

RECOMMENDED RESOURCES

Apps

- Pinterest is a great resource for meal ideas.
- TikTok has inspiration from vegan influencers to amazing home cooks.
- Instagram is a game-changer for meal suggestions.

Books

- Shop Smart by PJ Gray
- Better Groceries for Less Cash by Randall Putala
- Shop Smart and Eat Great by Taste of Home
- How to Save Money on Groceries without Coupons by Madeleine Wayfair

"Opportunity is missed
by most people because
it is dressed in overalls
and looks like work."
~ Thomas Edison

Saying YES to NO!

No and negativity have notoriously been linked together. Many people may not realize the damaging feelings they project when they receive a "no," including those of guilt, selfishness, and resentment. Saying "no" is essential to prioritize your life. You cannot be all things to all people. I am quick to say, *"I AM NOT EVERY WOMAN, IT'S NOT ALL IN ME!"*

Though there are perceived negative connotations behind it, saying no is an act of self-balance and confidence. Whether it's a straightforward no or a finessed decline, here are some ways to politely say no and preserve your personal or professional relationship[2].

- Sounds great, but I can't commit.
- No thank you, but it sounds lovely.
- I appreciate the offer, however…
- I'm grateful for the invitation, but I am completely booked.
- You're so kind to think of me, but I can't.
- I'm flattered you considered me, but unfortunately, I'll have to pass this time.
- Unfortunately, it's not a good time.
- I'm not taking on anything else right now.

- It's not feasible for me to take this on.
- I'm not really into it, but thanks for asking!
- I think I'll pass.
- Maybe another time.
- I have something else to do.
- No thanks, I won't be able to make it.
- No thanks, I have another commitment.
- I'm buckling down on my priorities, so I can't.
- I'm really spread thin, so I can't do it.
- I've got too much on my plate right now.
- My bandwidth is low, so I won't be able to.
- I really don't have any openings in my schedule.
- It doesn't sound like the right fit.

What are some other ways you can politely say no?

_____

_____

_____

_____

_____

_____

_____

_____

ACTION: SAY THESE AFFIRMING WORDS TO YOURSELF:

- I find my voice and tell *myself* NO.
- No, I will not ignore the red flags.
- No, I will not be their savior anymore.
- No, I will not answer that call.
- No, I will not loan more money.
- No, I will not support your GoFundMe.
- No, I will not help with this project.
- No, I will not work late.
- No, I will not attend the PTA function.
- No, I will not be cooking dinner tonight.

What are some additional NO's you can begin to implement?

_____

_____

_____

_____

_____

_____

_____

_____

_____

_____

TIPS

- For family members who don't have life insurance, consider getting a group of reliable family members to preemptively pool your resources together, each contributing $25 biweekly to cover the uninsured ones; this removes or greatly limits the GoFundMe requests. Additionally, it prevents hardened hearts, harsh words, and hurt feelings. Final funeral arrangements must be covered one way or the other so why not be proactive.

RECOMMENDED RESOURCE

Book

- [How to Say No Without Feeling Guilty](#) by Patti Breitman

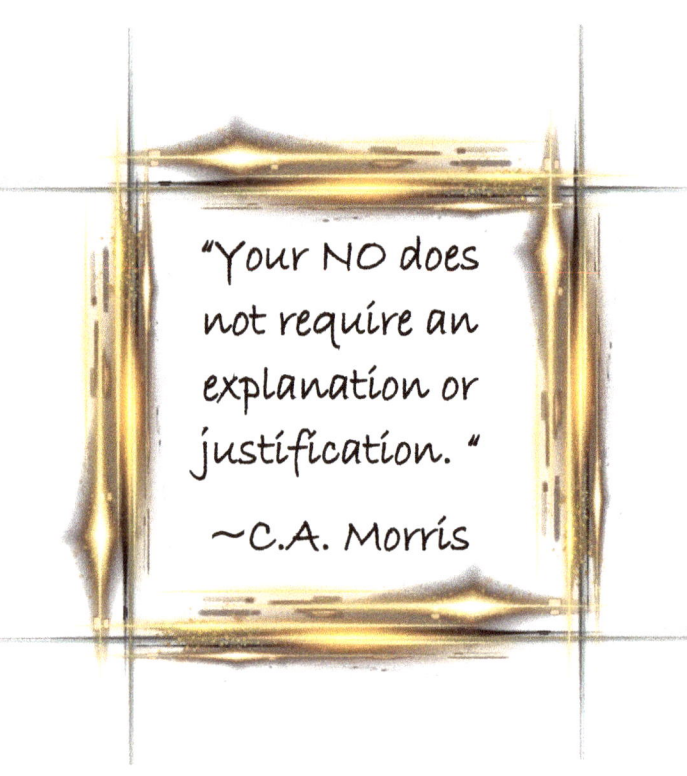

"Your NO does not require an explanation or justification."

~C.A. Morris

Financial Dream Team

If your tendency is to do things on your own, as you get it done faster or you don't like to depend on others, then you are working against yourself. Being a lone ranger is not a sustainable model for long-term success. And truth be told, the Lone Ranger did have Tonto.

There are dependable people who can help you achieve success and mitigate the risk of losing it. You do not have to do it alone. Ultimately, failure to grow your team of "me" can end up sabotaging your overall mission.

If you[3]?:

- Always think you can do it better than others
- Feel guilty letting go
- Feel threatened by other talented people
- Fear others who you use will mess up
- Often feel overwhelmed

Then you may be suffering from the Lone Ranger syndrome. To break out of this, build a team and delegate responsibilities to them. Trust that you've hired well and will not impede on their assignment by micromanaging them.

While on your way to destination manifestation, there are some key team members who can advise you on the best ways to protect yourself.

ACTIONS: When assembling your team[4], ask:

For Financial Advisors:

Will you be acting as my "fiduciary?"

_____
_____
_____

What's your money-management style?

_____
_____
_____

Have you ever been disciplined by a regulatory body?

_____
_____
_____

For Accountants:

Do you belong to professional groups requiring continuing education?

_____
_____
_____

Can you represent me in court if required?

_____
_____
_____

What is your audit record?

_____
_____
_____

For Lawyers:

Will you or your junior associate manage my matters?

_____
_____
_____

How do you charge? Per hour? Per session? Per transaction?

_____
_____
_____

What will the total cost be?

_____
_____
_____

TIPS

- Talk to multiple professionals for the service(s) you are looking to get to ensure you have the best fit for your needs.

- Ask for references from each person and then call the reference to hear about the services they've rendered

- Check the firm on the Better Business Bureau, Yelp, Google Reviews to see how they fare in the court of public opinion!

RECOMMENDED RESOURCES

Websites

- National Association of Personal Financial Advisors

- Certified Financial Planner Board of Standards

- Financial Planning Association

- Martindale-Hubbell (Yelp-like for attorneys)

"As a team...coming together is a beginning. Keeping together is progress. Working together is success."

~Henry Ford

Long Live Legacies

As you move towards financial freedom and build your empire, the notion of legacy should also be a part of your strategy. Building a legacy means establishing something that will be sustainable for generations to come. Whether it's real estate, an endowment, a business or a righteous cause, your legacy will be one that speaks for you long after you've transitioned.

ACTION: Answer the following questions.

If you had to do one thing to improve your world, what would your contribution be?

_____
_____
_____

What are you doing to impact the future for others?

_____
_____
_____

What do you desire your legacy to be? For what do you want to be remembered?

_____
_____
_____

Do you have a last will and testament, living trust and a living will in place? When was the last time you reviewed it?

_____

_____

_____

DOCUMENT FEATURES	Do Nothing - No Will or Trust	Last Will and Testament	Revocable Living Trust
Name beneficiaries for property	Government decides	Yes	Yes
Control distribution of assets	Government decides	Yes	Yes
Assets included	Yes	Only probate assets	Assets transferred to the trust
Leave property to young children	Government decides	No	Yes
Ability to revise your document	N/A	Yes	Yes
Requires transfer of property	Government decides	No	Yes
Protection from court challenges	No	No	Yes
Avoid a conservatorship	No	No	Yes
Names property manager for children's property	Government decides	No	Yes
Names an executor	Government decides	No	Yes
Instructs how taxes and debts should be paid	No	Yes	No
Requires witnesses	N/A	Yes	No
Requires a notary public	N/A	No	Yes
Effective date	N/A	At death	Immediately
Avoids probate	No	No	Yes*
Public record	Yes	Yes	No*
Creditors' claim	Yes	Limited time to file claims	Claims may be made at any time
Avoid estate taxes	No	No	No
Appoint guardian for minor-aged children	Government decides	Yes	No
Incapacity planning	No	No	Yes
Stipulations on inheritance	N/A	No	Yes

*Dependent on applicable State laws

Go to 21DaySpendingDetox.com to download a copy.

Have you listed what is of value to you and provided a copy to your trusted family member/friend/attorney?

_____

_____

_____

When was the last time you reviewed and updated your beneficiaries?

_____

_____

_____

How will you pass on your experience, knowledge, and skillset to the next generation?

_____

_____

_____

Does your business have a succession plan in place?

Assess	Identify	Prepare	Transition	Rebalance	Track (Continuously)
Assess the leadership demand required to achieve strategic goals	Identify succession candidates from internal and external pipelines	Prepare successors to meet evolving role requirements	Transition successors to new roles	Re-balance the leadership bench for long-term strategic relevance	Track the plan's success and execution and make adjustments accordingly

Source: Gartner (February 2019)

Go to 21DaySpendingDetox.com to download a copy.

_____

_____

TIP

- If you are unable to procure a lawyer to do your estate planning, use legal services like Legal Zoom, Legal Shield, or Rocket Lawyer. These services will walk you through creating documents and teach you how to ensure they are legally enforceable.

RECOMMENDED RESOURCES

Books

- Estate Planning 101 by Vicki Cook and Amy Blacklock
- Generational Wealth: Beginner's Business and Investing Guide by LaFoy Thomas III, Esq.

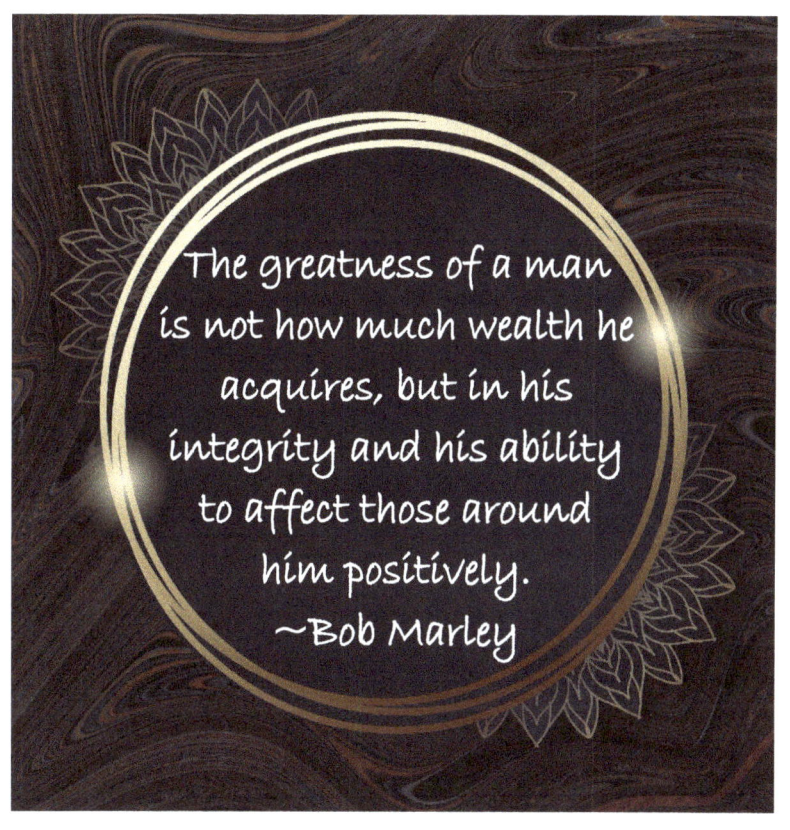

The greatness of a man is not how much wealth he acquires, but in his integrity and his ability to affect those around him positively.
~Bob Marley

21-DAY
SPENDING DETOX
Reset to Gain and Maintain Financial Freedom

CHARITY MORRIS

You can purchase the 21-Day Spending Detox book on www.21DaySpendingDetox.com.

You will be able to download the

21-Day Spending Detox App

September 2024.

Sign up at

www.21DaySpendingDetox.com

to receive updates.

REFERENCES

1. Financial Infidelity by Jini Thornton. © 2015. Retrieved December 15, 2021. https://6e553e7c-f697-46d7-879f-e6cf8c328338.filesusr.com/ugd/b87d69_00f9452fb8004628ba95b42a3ecfc9d3.pdf

2. How to Say No Without Feeling Guilty by Heather Moulder, J.D., ACC. © 2012. Retrieved on September 9, 2022. https://www.coursecorrectioncoaching.com/say-no-without-feeling-guilt/

3. 5 Signs You're a Lone Ranger Leader by Carey Nieuwhof. © 2022

4. How to Build Your Financial Dream Team by Karen Blumenthal. © 2011. Retrieved January 8, 2022. https://www.wsj.com/articles/SB10001424052970204296804577124662217267128

www.ingramcontent.com/pod-product-compliance
Lightning Source LLC
Chambersburg PA
CBHW051215120626
46547CB00013B/1360